This

Finding Who You are and What You Want

Phillip Brunnengraeber

Cover Photo by: Kiel Maddox

Dedication

To my students. Teaching you has been an absolute joy for well over a decade now. I absolutely love working with you and I hope that in some small way I may have helped nurture some growth in you that has helped you become the amazing people you are and will be. I look forward to continuing to watch all of you bloom. Much love.

Forward

First of all, I'm super excited that you're reading this because it means you're interested in personal growth and being a better version of you! It also means that I am helping someone live their authentic life and that brings me tremendous joy. Life is a journey with plenty of highs and lows but what's most important is that we grow and embrace who we are in this world and that's what this book is all about.

So, what is "*This is Crazy*?" After years of teaching, coaching kids, raising my own children, I decided that helping people beyond my classroom is something that would bring me a lot of joy. So, I began this venture into Life Coaching. I went with the brand "This is Crazy," because I honestly say it all the time and the world is crazy! People are crazy! Kids are crazy! Nature is crazy! Everything is crazy! I mean it in an adventurous and wonderous way and so it is meant to be light hearted.

This is the first of my efforts to create a book to help people in my coaching efforts, but I have many more planned. My areas of expertise are certainly kids and young people, parenting, relationships, recovering from abuse and neglecting and of course general growth and inspiration. I am looking forward to many years of helping many people. Thank you for being along for the adventure.

Introduction

I'll be perfectly honest. It's taken me some time to learn some things I ought to have known. I've not been especially successful in some areas of my life. I'm divorced twice before I even turn forty, in spite of the fact that I love being married and very much want a partner. I am a teacher, and although I feel I'm a good one, I've had days where I literally put on a video because I had no lesson and no energy to create one. I'm a dad, and an awesome one, but I've for sure lost my patience and snapped at my kids. I'm a writer, but you won't see my books anywhere near the bestseller list. Do I wish I was crushing it from my early 20s and had all I want in life? Of course. But I didn't. I failed along the way and each failure brought with it more lessons. I finally feel I've reached the point where I know who I am as a person and what I want in life, and that has been huge. The journey has been difficult at times, but I've continued to move forward and strive to improve, and I'm thrilled to be where I am.

So that's where this project comes in. I decided that when I looked at my skills, abilities, experience and passion, that helping people is directly in the center of my heart. It's why I became a teacher, it's what I love about being a dad. It's why I joined the army and why I loved serving in 4-H. I enjoy helping people and this is another way I can widen my circle of influence and reach more people. I'm an encourager by nature and generally try to laugh my way through life's difficulties. The world can be a crazy place and it can seem overwhelming often, but plenty of people have thrived and any of us can with only some minor changes. That's what this is about. That's what the goal of *This is Crazy!* is all about. I want you to thrive in a world that can and does swallow people up.

I'm not necessarily that special. In fact, I like to think that I'm like most people. I've been in bad relationships. I've made mistakes. I've even hurt people with my choices. At times I've been too selfish. At other times I've been too selfless and been taken advantage of. I've felt lost. I've felt unstoppable. I've been through some really dark and low points and I've also had some fantastic moments that I cherish. If there is something that might set me apart from some, perhaps it is my ability to form all those experiences and feelings into a narrative and a lesson that can enrich the lives of other people. So there we go. I'm just like you, I just talk more and I'm going to share with you some of the things I learned and experienced in the hope that you will benefit and that together we can thrive even more than we already are!

As a history teacher, I cannot help myself. When you read the poems and tales of the Ancient Greeks, they are rich with lessons and symbolism. One of the most profound lessons found in them was the story of Socrates and his trip to the Oracle at Delphi. If you don't know, Socrates was considered one of the wisest men of the time and indeed of all time. Not surprisingly however, his wisdom and propensity to constantly challenge people's ideas got him into a lot of trouble. He was eventually ordered exiled from Athens but because he was stubborn and a bit of a punk, he chose death instead. He told a tale of his trip to seek wisdom from an Oracle. When he asked the Oracle for wisdom, the Oracle told him "be true to yourself." This message was repeated in Shakespeare's Hamlet "to thine own self be true," which sounds much cooler, obviously. Maybe it sounds even more awesome in the original Greek but I don't speak ancient Greek so I'm not sure.

The point is this, if you do not have a strong sense of self, you won't function especially well. You are far less likely to be happy in anything if you don't even know yourself well. You'll be less likely to get what you want, be with someone who is good for you or even get a career or job that is satisfying if you don't know yourself well. When we are not true to our authentic selves, we feel uneasy and strangely dissatisfied. Often times we cannot even put our fingers on what is wrong we just know something is off. Believe me, I've been there. It took me a while, but I can finally say I know exactly who I am and exactly what I want in life. That isn't to say I'm not still learning and growing; I certainly am, but it is to say that when I got to know who I was, what I wanted became clearer and when I started living true to me, then I had joy like never before. If that's what you want, then you're in the right place. Let's go on a journey of self discovery together and find that place of peace and joy within you.

Chapter One: Who am I and What do I Want?

Not a Tank Driver

Like most kids, I changed my mind on what I wanted to be "when I grow up" all the time. Naturally I wanted to be everything at one point. For some reason I definitely thought I was going to be a paleontologist for a couple years at least. Dinosaurs were huge in the 80s and 90s and the word paleontologist sounded amazing. It wasn't until later that I discovered that they mostly dug around in the Utah desert and made little to no money, but that wasn't even the breaking point for me. I grew up with Brontosaurus being one of the big three dinosaurs (along with T-Rex and triceratops). Then one day I read that they had mixed up the bones of a pair of other dinosaurs and there was never any such animal called a Brontosaurus. So scientists with a super fancy name mixed up bones and named a creature that never existed and I had that fake thing on my T-shirts, lunch pail and on posters in my room? Nope, I was done with paleontology. Sounded like a sham to me.

I bounced around from wanting to be a pharmacist at one point because I heard they made $35,000 a year which seemed like a lot, to wanting to be a lawyer. Of course, my family backed me up with the lawyer idea because it probably seemed prestigious to them and lawyers are believed to make a lot of money even though only a few do. But in the end I decided I didn't want to do that either. Like most 17 year olds, I didn't really know what the heck I wanted to do. Honestly, I work with more than 200 of them a year as a teacher and even the ones who know what they want to do will change their minds because, well, they're only 17! It's nuts to think you know what you want to do with the rest of your life at only 17. Some do and that's great for them, but most don't.

So, with my parents getting divorced and completely broke, and me not having any idea what I really wanted to do with myself, I decided to join the army. Why not? It would get me away from an environment that wasn't especially conducive to growth and would be a great opportunity to do some new things and meet some new people. Plus, they were offering college money when I got out if I even did decide what they heck I wanted to do with myself. This was one of the very first authentic choices I made for myself in my life and it felt fantastic!

I met with the recruiter many times, he came over to the house and had to talk to my parents since I wasn't 18 yet. My dad was all for it. He had dreams of being in the navy and for some reason wasn't true to himself and was living vicariously through me. My mom on the other hand, was completely against it. She told me I was too weak to be in the army and would get killed. She tried everything she could to stop me from making this, my first authentic decision. I was angry and deeply hurt that she would actively try to discourage me and even tell me such negative messages just for her own selfish motives. In the end she signed. The damage done to our relationship lasted years.

I was shipped off to get a medical examine and if I passed that, to finally enlist in the US Army! I passed my medical examine although I had some difficulty peeing in a cup with a grown man staring directly at the, ah, cup, but once I overcame that challenge, it was on to the career counselor's office!

A high ranking sergeant was seated with a computer when I was called in and asked me what I wanted to be. I enthusiastically answered, "I want to drive a tank!"

That is precisely what I wanted to do by the way. After all, I was 17, my mom told me I was weak, and I watched Abrams tanks roll across the desert of Kuwait in Desert Storm when I was a kid. It seemed totally awesome. I wanted to do that.

The sergeant looked at something for a moment and told me, "We don't have that job right now."

I was devastated. I wanted to drive a tank. I came to the only place I could think of that had tanks. I took a written test, spread my butt cheeks for a doctor, peed in a cup with a grown man watching and now I find out they don't have tank driving jobs? Brutal.

The sergeant added, "Do you like foreign language?"

You see, he had all the information I just listed, and he knew I had a really high written score and I'm just guessing that he didn't have too many recruits coming in there with scores like that and he could find plenty of guys to drive a tank so he offered something else.

I nodded and answered, "I'm in my fourth year of German."

"Ah! How would you like to be a linguist?"

I didn't know what a linguist was. I mean, I didn't know what an army linguist did, anyways. He said I would have to take another test. I agreed. Long story short, that's how I became a linguist for the US Army. Those were some of the best days of my young life. It turned out that being a linguist was awesome and I embraced it fully as well as being a soldier. I made great friends, I had great times, and I had great experiences. I was living my authentic self then and everything was going well. That's my goal for you. To find your authentic self.

Are you doing what you want?

It's common knowledge that a huge number of people are unhappy. It may be that they are unhappy with their jobs or their relationships or politics or whatever, but we all know that there are plenty of unhappy people out there. Yet, we're all trying to improve that state. Or at least say we are. Something like more than 90% of people do not achieve their New Year's resolution. Something like 70% of people are unhappy in their job or career. More than half of marriages end in divorce. So much failure out there! So much unhappiness! What is the root cause of it all? Is it really society that is keeping us down? The 1%? The Illuminati? Maybe the answer is inside us all along.

What do you tell people if they ask you to talk about yourself? Do you tell them about your relationship? Your job? Probably right? When asked about who we are we often default to describing things external from ourselves and not internal characteristics. Do we tell people what we like? Or the type of person we are? Not likely. We are far more likely to give people descriptions of what we do or who we associate with. But those things are NOT who we are. Who we are is much deeper than that. Who we are means what things we think about when we are alone. Who we are is how we feel when things happen and the emotions we experience throughout the day. Those things are far more consequential when we discuss who we are than what we do for money or who our family is.

So who are you? What makes you tick? What do you dream about? Those are the things you will have to focus on before you can even decide whether you're being true to yourself. Those were the things I had to figure out before I knew whether I was living my life for me or for other people.

One of the things I finally knew and embraced was how much I love writing. Sure, I haven't really made any money at it, and for some reason, the partners I've had, have put me down for it and discouraged me, but when I embraced that I just love it and I'm going to do it because it makes me happy, I was at peace. Now, writing is a very regular part of my life. Whether its stories or poems or some satirical article I'm writing, being able to express myself and what I'm feeling through writing with no guilt or shame has helped me embrace my true self. This is even more evidence that I'm living that authentic self and I'm happy even writing this now. You too can have that level of joy and peace by embracing who you are.

When we embrace who we are and who we're meant to be, all other things come into alignment and we find peace. It may take some time and there may be some mistakes along the way, but the work is well worth it to find who you are and then what you really want. I support you on this journey and others will too; if they actually care about your joy and peace.

How do I know?

Now you need to spend some time considering the questions raised in this chapter. Do you know who you really are? If you do, do you know what you want? If you actually think you do, then I want you to consider whether everything is working for you and if it isn't then perhaps you're missing something. In my experience, the people who have a really good sense of self and know what they want, typically get it. So, if you're coming up short in some way, then it may do you well to consider that something may be missing.

But how? Think of a time when you were really happy. You know, those days when you're sitting there at the end and smiling, and people wonder what's wrong with you and you can't answer especially clearly but you know you're happy; content. Those are the moments when you're living your authentic real life. The life you are meant to live. Think about at least one of those times. What were you doing? Where were you? Who were you with? All those things are factors in contributing to your inner peace and joy. Any one of them can either improve or destroy your peace. Write them down. Can you think of another time? Write that one down. And another. Is there a pattern there? If there is then you're on the right track to finding out the things that bring you peace and joy.

Now do the opposite. Think of a time when you were absolutely miserable. I'm not talking about just having a bad day. I'm talking about a time when you were sitting there thinking that nothing could get worse and you couldn't possibly feel any worse than you were in that moment. This part of the exercise is possibly even more important since it's probably easier to remember. Our brains have a built-in survival mechanism that strives to keep us alive and when we feel miserable we often try to avoid that in future. What was going on? Who was there? Where were you? All those details are likely hints to who you are and what you want in life. Think of another time and another. You may begin to see a pattern develop.

If it isn't clear now it's ok. Over the course of the next few chapters we are going to work on finding your authentic self and embracing that you. Then we'll work on identifying what you want and then working towards those goals. The more work you put in now the further you will get but we make progress no matter what. It's going to be awesome and I'm excited for you.

Review
- The pursuit of our true self is one of the greatest and most fulfilling aims we can have
- Most people do not have a good sense of self
- Most people are miserable in aspects of their lives
- In this course, you will identify who you are
- In this course, you will discover what you want
- By the end of the course you will be on the path to embracing who you are and what makes you happy

Self-Work:
Work on identifying the times you were truly at peace and describe them in as much detail as possible. Try to identify the times you were uneasy and unhappy and describe them in as much detail as possible. Take your time. Days if you

need. But write about times when you were really happy and content. When everything seemed right. Then do the same with times you felt everything was miserable and nothing was ever going to be good again.

Chapter Two: Where did You Come From?

Drill Sergeant Drama

How about another army story? Basic training was, at that point, the most difficult challenge of my life. It was physically exhausting but beyond that, it was mentally and emotionally draining. That was on purpose of course as the military sought to take people from all over the country and even US territories and forge us all into a fighting force prepared to meet all enemies, foreign and domestic. It was intense most days and ultimately very rewarding.

We were divided into companies and four platoons per company of 40 soldiers each. I was in 1st platoon. The drill Sergeants for 1st platoon were: Drill Sergeant Farmer, an African American woman, Drill Sergeant Lopez a short stocky Hispanic man, and Drill Sergeant Lichenauer a monster of a white man with no neck and arms that did not fold to his side on account of their enormous size.

Drill sergeants were trained to mess with soldiers. It was an art form and they were masters of it. They constantly attacked your identity as they sought to destroy it and replace it with one that suited their needs and they were highly skilled in this regard. One day, not long into training, Drill Sergeant Lopez got in my face, hitting his round brown hat against the bridge of my nose and asked me where I was from.

I promptly answered, "California."

Lopez continued to taunt me in his raspy voice that sounded like he took shrapnel to the throat at one point, "Oh, you must be from Humboldt."

For those of you who aren't familiar, Humboldt county is in the Northern part of California and is known for marijuana plantations and significant consumption to boot.

"No Drill Sergeant," I answered respectfully. "I'm from Fresno."

"I bet you smoke a little Humboldt too don't you?"

"No Drill Sergeant, I've never touched it."

"Oh, I see, had someone else roll it then?" Classic Drill Sergeant burn! Obviously, I was from California so I must smoke weed. Unoriginal, but still funny.

Later, Drill Sergeant Lichenaur, who had been missing for most of our cycle because he was training, showed up to introduce himself to us. Honestly, he was terrifying. His face was either acne scared, or he washed it with gravel because it was worn like bark on an old tree.

We were all seated and he began to address us, introducing himself to us and apparently prepared to give us some sort of motivational speech. He immediately asked where Private Brunnengraeber was. That's me. I was frozen in fear but popped to my feet, snapped to parade rest and answered, "Here, Drill Sergeant."

He asked, "Are you German, son?"

"Yes, Drill Sergeant."

"Drop."

"Drop" means to do push-ups. I was super confused. I had never met this man before. I had only seen him a couple of times. I could not understand why he picked me out. I mean, obviously, my name is super German, and in fact my grandparents are from Germany, and his name is also super German and perhaps he was the result of some sort of Nazi experiments which is why he lacked a neck and had arms like trees, but it didn't make sense otherwise.

Lichenaur then proceeded to give a lecture on how he doesn't discriminate against anyone. I was more confused. Hadn't he just told me to do push-ups because my name is German? He continued for a while, but I wasn't really listening. I was trying to figure out what was going on. He dismissed everyone but told me to stay. He ordered me to get up and get in what they called the "detox" position against a tree.

The "detox" position is when you lean against the tree or whatever with your legs bent at a 90-degree angle and your arms out. It is easy enough to hold for a minute but gets exhausting pretty fast. I don't really recall what he was telling me or asking me, but I do remember him telling me I was weak, and I wasn't going to make it in "his army." It was always "their" army somehow and the Drill Sergeants acted like it was their mission to get rid of people not fit to serve. Maybe it was in fact their mission.

It didn't end there. Every time Drill Sergeant Lichenaur showed up, he singled me out. Many in the rest of the platoon began to ask me what the heck was going on and I honestly had no answer whatsoever. I couldn't for the life of me figure out what I had done to deserve his attention.

Finally, one day we were practicing Drill and Ceremony nearing the completion of our training and Lichenaur showed up to chat with Drill Sergeant Farmer for a minute. At the end of their conversation he was walking away but then remembered he hadn't tortured me yet. He turned and immediately asked if I was there. I answered that I was and when he ordered me to fall out of formation and come to him. I didn't hesitate. Whatever his game was, I was determined to meet him face to face.

This time I had my M-16 rifle with me. No, this isn't going to turn into *Full Metal Jacket*. He told me to do a "military press" with my rifle which is an exercise that involves lifting the rifle up over your head, out in front of you and over your head again. Something snapped in me. I don't really recall again what he was telling me, but it involved more taunting and negative messaging. I was determined to continue to do the exercise and whatever else he demanded of me till he was either satisfied that I had proved his negative messages wrong, or collapsed.

A surge of adrenaline pumped through my body and I began to push harder and faster. By then I had already gained significant muscle after two months of training and I was capable of continuing for a while. I pumped my arms and felt my strength and I smiled. He continued to taunt me, but I ignored it and exercised. With still no idea why he picked me out except that my name is German, I was not going to let him beat me. After a while, he ordered me to stop and to return to my training. I shouted, "Yes Drill Sergeant!" and ran back to formation. All my platoon mates were watching and I had a huge smile on my face when I got back in line with sweat pouring down my face. He never singled me out again until he awarded me a coin for being the most motivated soldier during our final training exercise.

The point is this, our past absolutely has an impact on who we are. Our name, or ethnicity our past choices all have some sort of impact, but they do not have to define us. We can push through those preconceived notions people have about us and achieve whatever we want. We can't control how people see us, but we absolutely control who we really are. With that in mind, let's dive into our past and see what it is that is weighing us down.

What did you do?

I'm going to go out on a limb and guess that we all have things we would love to change about our past. Maybe you did something wrong. Maybe you hurt someone. Maybe you didn't stick up for a friend when you should have or maybe you lied about something and it bothers you. Unless you're a narcissist, (and I've known a few of them) we all have things we regret.

What's worse, maybe you are ashamed of where you came from. Maybe you wished your family had more money or maybe you wish you were a different race. I see it all the time, honestly. Again, I teach more than 200 students a year in a very diverse school district and I come across students all the time who don't match the stereotypical cultural norms of their race. And sadly, mirroring the culture of another group tends to put you at odds with both your own culture group and the one you prefer. But I'm not here to tell you what to do except to tell you to be your authentic self. If you're a person who feels more comfortable around people different ethnically from you then continue to be you. It doesn't matter at the end of the day which group you are as long as you're being true to you.

If I'm being honest, I kinda wish I was Hispanic. As a white kid with a super fractured family there were not many family events that I got to enjoy. My Hispanic neighbors have family events constantly. I long for that. Plus, there is always beer and I love beer. My best friend growing up was from a Mexican family and I learned quickly that no matter if I had already eaten, his mom was going to make me a plate, and when I left, I was going to take a plate of food home. I absolutely love this about Hispanic culture. I'm white, mixed with more white, but at heart I feel at home in the family oriented Hispanic families with lots of food and beer. Be authentic.

So, what's holding you back then? What is it that you need to come to terms with? I assure you that there is nothing in your past that has to define your future indefinitely. We've all made mistakes; some worse than others but we've all done it. I wish I wasn't divorced twice. I wish I hadn't been a part of a super abusive marriage (my second one). I wish my dad hadn't died so young. I wish I hadn't messed up so many things, but I have processed those things and forgiven myself. Let's do it together for you. You'll feel much lighter and the weight of your past won't be carried into your much brighter future. It may not happen right away, but it will happen as long as you're committed to growing and being a better more authentic version of you. Let's go.

How do I let go of past mistakes?

If you haven't embraced it already, I need you to know how absolutely important this part is. You cannot carry with you the burdens of your past. You have got to let go if you want to move forward. I know it isn't easy, but if you are letting those things define you, then you can't be the awesome you, you are meant to be.

Think of something you regret or have shame about. Maybe, if you are afraid of this process, pick something smaller to start. Maybe you got in trouble as a kid or made some sort of mistake that is pretty common. I know I drank underaged multiple times and got myself into a little trouble and I shouldn't have. Find something you know you can let go of.

Next, after you identified the thing that you regret, think about specifically what it is about it that bothers you. For me, when I was young and drinking, I sometimes said things I regret that were rude or mean and once I even got wrapped up into a situation in which the police intervened. It was really stupid. I was making poor choices and was allowing peers to influence me into acting differently than my authentic self. What is it specifically that you regret about the situation?

Now that you know exactly why it bothers you so much, now I want you to think about what you should have done instead. Obviously, I should not have drank nearly as much or as often as I was. I don't like being drunk to the point at which I am not really in control of myself and I'm no longer acting like my real, authentic self. So, I should have done something different. I should have either said no to drinking altogether or I should have stopped before I was too intoxicated. What should you have done? What would you do differently now? What I mean is, if you were behaving like your true self, the self you love, what would you do? Imagine the situation over again and imagine the decision you would make now. That's who you are. You made a mistake, but you do not have to let that mistake define you.

Now, and this is very important, take responsibility for that mistake. Own it. You did it. I did it. We messed up. Everyone does. Maybe someone was even hurt by what you or I did. Apologize to them if you haven't already. Explain that you regret it and that if you could do it over again you would do it differently. Tell yourself as well because in the end you have to believe it more than anyone else. Others may or may not believe you, it doesn't matter if they do. You have to take responsibility for your own sake first. Being accountable is foundational to being your authentic self.

Lastly, forgive yourself. Really forgive yourself. Tell yourself you're sorry you messed up. Tell yourself you're sorry for the hurt you caused. Tell yourself you're sorry for the pain you caused and most importantly, tell yourself you're sorry for not being true to you. You betrayed your real self and you're sorry. Cry if you have to. Get angry if you have to. Take as much time as you need. But forgive yourself fully. You have to let it go or this regret will keep you from being who you really are. You cannot let a mistake or two or two hundred define you. If you cannot let go then stop. There's no point in going forward to finding who you really are and seeking what you really want if you cannot forgive yourself for past mistakes. Let go and commit to being better. That's all we can do. But we must do it.

Now, if the things you regret are not choices you made, if the pain and hurt was caused by someone else, and outside of your control then this is even easier. You didn't do it. It was done to you and it isn't your fault. In that case, forgive yourself for letting those wounds or those circumstances control you. Then let go. You have to let go. You cannot let the binds that others place on you keep you from becoming your real self. You cannot be bound by any external forces. Your race doesn't matter, your ethnicity doesn't matter, your sexuality doesn't matter, your gender doesn't matter, your religion doesn't matter, none of that matters when it comes to being who you really are and loving yourself. Let all those things go. You do NOT need anyone else's permission or approval or affirmation to be yourself. You have all the affirmation you need inside you. You are all the love you need. You MUST let go of any negative messages or labels others put on you. Just like I learned to fight against the negative messages my mom told me about not being strong enough that were only reinforced by a crazy Drill Sergeant, you have the power in you to be exactly who you want to be, and no one can stop you. Forgive yourself for ever letting anyone else define you and let go of that negativity.

Now that you know the process and you've already let go of something and forgiven yourself, do it again with anything still weighing you down. You have to find all those things in your past that keep you from moving forward and work through them. If they are too big and you find that you need help, that's ok too. I needed help to sort through some of the hurt and pain I carried with me. I highly recommend that you seek the help of a counselor or therapist if you find you cannot work through some of your negative self-images and regrets. There is no rush and we are all on our own path at our own pace. You'll find that when you can get some of those major blocks out of the way, your growth will explode! You'll suddenly see things in a new way and understand things you never thought possible. The world will make much more sense and you'll be much happier being your true self. And if you struggle with addiction of some sort then, again, I highly recommend seeking professional help to overcome whatever it is that is holding you down. You owe it to yourself. The world will still be there when you're healed and ready to conquer it. I promise.

Review
- Everyone has made mistakes and done things that were not true to their authentic self
- We cannot move forward with being our best version of our self if we allow our past to define us
- We must take responsibility for the mistakes we've made and the hurts we've caused
- We must forgive ourselves for things we regret and let go
- We have all the affirmation and love we need and do NOT have to seek it from others

Self-Work:

Identify the things that you regret that are holding you back. Work through them individually, taking responsibility and forgiving yourself. Identify any labels that might be making your identity inauthentic and forgive yourself for letting them do so.

Continue to work through any regrets until you are free from the burdens of your past. Seek professional help for anything that you cannot resolve yourself.

Begin by making a list of things that bother you or mistakes you've made that you haven't forgiven yourself for. Summarize what happened. Describe what you did wrong. Write about what you should have done. Then forgive yourself. Write your forgiveness out too so you can review it if you're still having trouble letting go. Then repeat the process for all the things you feel are still weighing on you.

Once you've gone through mistakes you feel you made, do the same for things that happened to you. Summarize the event if you are able but you must forgive yourself. Tell yourself it wasn't your fault. You need to process those things. Keep going until you've unloaded the burden that our wounds are to us.

Lastly, if there is anything about your identity that you feel you're not comfortable with, spend some time writing out your affirmation. Write a letter to yourself telling you how awesome you are and how wonderful your identity is and also how it doesn't change anything if others don't view you as amazing as you view you. You're all you need. Love yourself and be awesome; because you are.

Chapter Three: What am I doing?

Don't tell mom

We sometimes, no let me make this stronger, we always develop some beliefs along the way that are not always true and do not serve us well as adults trying to be as awesome and happy as we can. Some of them we learn from our parents or our family, others are from experiences that were either positive or negative but were likely connected with a strong feeling.

For example, if you really had a crush on someone as a kid, and you were infatuated with them. You thought about them all the time. You drew little pictures or wrote little things about them, maybe you made hearts with your names in them. You get the point, you were really into them. Then one day, you got up the courage to tell them. Maybe you drew them something, made a card, or wrote a poem or any of the odd yet romantic gestures we do to show someone we care. But, to your horror, they rejected you. Hopefully they did it in a kind manner but it's also possible they were cruel about it; too young to be able to empathize with your feelings. If that happened, you were probably crushed. You may have felt like there was no reason to continue on living. I'm sure it felt like the world had ended. It did not end after all, but that experience may have created a belief in you that you carry to this day. You may have believed from that day forward that people do not want to be with you. Maybe you believed that love was a waste of time. Maybe you believed you were not good enough, not attractive enough, not worthy of love. Maybe you decided that being romantic was dumb and a waste of time.

With beliefs like those, which we all pick up at some point, we forge ahead in life but with a different and somewhat inaccurate view of the world and ourselves. We may abandon all hope of love and be very bitter about it. Or we may try again but this time, lower our standards and get into relationships with any who will take us regardless of what we want and regardless of whether we are happy. I've for sure been there. Many of us have.

But even success can create false beliefs. I see it a ton with gifted kids in school. Giftedness in academics typically is applied to a student who is especially quick to process information and learns quickly; making connections and solving problems better than most. These students are the ones who grow up getting strong grades, sometimes without much effort. The problem I battle with these students at the high school level, is that because school has been easy for them, they believe it always will be. But this is a false belief. While, yes, most things academically have been easy for them, there is always going to be a subject or a class that is challenging and when they hit that wall where it doesn't just click for them, their belief is challenged. Unfortunately, our ego tends to be pretty strong so when our beliefs are challenged, we like to dismiss the challenge, ignore the challenge or even attack it as unfair or just plain wrong. Often times, these super bright students do not try to master the challenge because it would mean, in their minds, that they are not as bright as they believed. Many of our brightest students are failing courses because they do not push themselves, put their ego aside, and accept that they will find things that are not easy for them. My job is to get them to let go of the belief that everything is easy and grow.

To put it another way, whatever beliefs we've been running around with, they will get in the way when we are trying to grow and be better. If you believe that no one will ever love you and you're not worthy of love, then your chance of finding satisfying love is miniscule. If you believe that everything in life is going to be easy for you, and when it isn't, the world is wrong, then you too are going to be very limited in your growth because the world is filled with challenges no matter how talented we may be naturally.

I've found a number of limiting beliefs that were holding me back in a number of ways in my own life. One that finally hit me one day was a belief that my father taught me. Bless him, and rest his soul, my father had a number of limiting beliefs and in spite of his superior intellect and incredible work ethic, the man lacked confidence and was very risk averse. He also tended to avoid conflict whenever possible. One of the things that he taught me was that it was much better to suppress your own feelings rather than confront a person who is causing you negative emotions. He was especially likely to do this with my mother. He actively coached me to be deceptive rather than honest and deal with the consequences of an action or decision.

For example, my father tended to drive ridiculously run down and poorly operating vehicles. We didn't have much money so that was part of it, but he also seemed to relish the fact that he could work on the vehicles although he didn't appear to be that talented at it. Regardless, his cars broke down a lot. More than once, when he would run out of gas or his car would break down, he would tell me to not tell my mother because she would get angry. He was right, she would get angry and often I heard those fights and they were a complete waste of time and only drove a wedge between them rather than brought them closer as they sought solutions as a team. She would yell at him and put him down until he finally got mad, kicked something or broke something then stormed out, driving away and not returning for hours.

There's a lot wrong with all of that, believe me, I know. But I want to focus on his belief that it would be better to just deceive his wife and have his son participate in the deception in order to avoid conflict. That is a TERRIBLE thing to do. Was there going to be a conflict? Of course! Was it going to be productive? Not a chance. But he needed to address their relationship, financial problems and the issue of unreliable transportation, and by being deceptive, they avoided the real problem and just created a false belief.

Sadly, I carried that belief into my first marriage. My default when I thought that there was going to be a conflict that I wasn't going to enjoy was to try to keep the information from her in the first place. It was not good in many ways. I suffered for years in silence, not bringing my hurts, pains, wants or needs to my spouse and she was shocked to find that I was absolutely miserable in our relationship when I was finally honest near its end. Had I been honest immediately, from the beginning, we would have had the opportunity to either deal with how I felt and what I wanted and ensure I was satisfied in the marriage or split up sooner than 13 years into a life together. I deeply regret how much pain that unhealthy belief caused to several people; including myself.

If it hasn't been made clear yet, let me state it again, identifying beliefs you hold about yourself, family, friends, your work or even the world, that are keeping you from being the best you possible is critical. You must find what it is you believe, and the actions connected to those beliefs, that are holding you back. You have the power to change those beliefs and replace them with healthier more empowering beliefs, but you must be honest with yourself and take a very long and hard look in the mirror.

What's holding you back?

We all have limiting belief in our lives that are holding us back from greatness. They are going to be very different depending on your own experience and life to this point but we have to get them out of the way so we can grow. So how do we find them?

They're easy enough to find if we take a step back and look closely. What are the areas that you are not happy with? There may be several, and there probably should be if you are really interested in long term growth, but find one to start. It could be about relationships, or work. Maybe you're not happy with finances or maybe you hate the neighborhood or home you live in. It can be something social or something tangible, but we all typically have areas that we want to improve in.

Take your time. Write them down. Now, you probably have one that jumps out at you. We typically have something causing us more stress than everything else and that issue is probably one we are not very successful in and there is probably a strong belief there that is creating a problem, but there are more. Journaling is a great way to identify the areas you want to improve but even just talking to close and trusted friends or family may also help, but beware, they may have contributed to the belief that is holding you back. Sometimes even those who love us and want what's best for us give us terrible advice or help us build awful beliefs that hold us back.

Don't tell me you don't have any area with a limiting belief either. You know one I see all the time? "I'm not good at math." I hate this one. I don't even teach math but I get so frustrated because so many students and adults believe this. But it's ridiculous. You aren't bad at math. You don't practice it, and you have a limiting belief about math. Let me prove this to you with a fantastic metaphor.

Math is not the easiest subject we teach kids. Other things seem to come somewhat easier and many subjects are information based (social science, life science) and not skills based like math or English Language Arts (writing essays as such). So, guess which subjects students tend to think they aren't good at? The skills based subjects. But we don't apply the understanding we have regarding skills in other areas to school.

Almost everyone can walk and do some basic physical activity. In the same way, we all have some basic ability to problem solve and do some logical reasoning. Before you disagree, if you can count and do some basic addition then you too have some ability in math. But even though we can all walk and perform some physical tasks, it doesn't mean we are all Olympic athletes. We don't all run marathons. But few of us go around saying, "I'm not good at running." We mostly acknowledge that we just hate running; that we choose not to run but that if we really wanted to, we could get better at running and even have some level of success running. Don't challenge me on this before looking on Facebook and seeing all the people on there completing 5Ks, running and getting fit. You can do it too if you wanted. I saw a video of a man with cerebral-palsy lifting 200 pounds. Make excuses if you like but you're only hurting yourself.

The point is this, we say "I'm not good at math," but what we really mean is that we have never put in the time and practice to master the skills necessary to be good at it. If we put more effort in, we would have better results.

This is the same with anything in our lives. We have things we haven't been successful in, but that doesn't mean we just aren't good at them. We can all be more successful with improved effort and by eliminating limiting beliefs.

An easy one for me was relationships. I was married 13 years and was miserable at the end of it and got out. I took a step back to try to find what I was doing wrong. There's the key too, don't try to blame your lack of success on something external or someone else, find what you can do better. Believe me, there were plenty of things I could have done better in that relationship. So, bear with me as I take you through the process with myself as an example.

How to change limiting beliefs

Step one for changing limiting beliefs is, identify a problem. Now, we struggle with this sometimes because we get stuck on how we feel and it's difficult to get to why. I felt unhappy and unsatisfied in a committed relationship. Ok, but why? For years I didn't know. I would complain and grumble and be unhappy, but I didn't really know why. Finally, it clicked. I wanted to do things, but I wasn't. What I mean is, there were a lot of things I wanted to be doing with my life that I wasn't. The passions the desires the curiosity I had, I intentionally suppressed in favor of what my partner wanted. So, I was dissatisfied because there were things I wanted to do and I wanted to live my life and spend my time in ways that were different from the way I was. That will do it every time by the way. As I stated in an earlier lesson, not living your authentic life will make you very miserable.

Perfect, so I was unhappy because I wasn't living the life I wanted. Step two, why was I not living the life I wanted? In other words, what was the belief that was keeping me from being happy and living the life I wanted? This is where it gets a little more interesting and difficult. I found that I wasn't living the life I wanted because I was intentionally giving into what my wife wanted in order to avoid conflict, just like my dad taught me.

Now, just like he taught me, I would try to get my needs met and live the life I wanted on the sly and keep it from her but that was neither fulfilling and was actually counter to my authentic self because I value honesty and I was being deceitful instead. I was only making myself more miserable because not only was I now violating my own values, but I was still not living the life I wanted to live.

I would play some video games when she wasn't around, or I would try to write when I had some extra time and would beg to play golf with my dad and jump through whatever hoops she put up for me to do so but this all made it worse. I should have told my wife what I wanted and then we could have compromised, and if she was unwilling to compromise to my reasonable requests then I would either do what I wanted and deal with the consequences of that or reconsider the relationships. But lying and still not living the life I wanted was not helping anyone.

So that's part of step three; adopt a better belief. When I realized that I wasn't getting what I wanted and wasn't living my authentic life, and that my own belief of suppressing what I wanted and lying to avoid conflict was a huge contributing factor, I had to make a change. I began to express what I wanted and be more authentic. It wasn't received especially well and ultimately, I ended that relationship. Over the last few years I've become much better at it and I love it! That's the final step.

Step four, practice the new belief. You have to practice the new belief. Now, to be honest, I got into a way unhealthy relationship after that marriage and it was abusive in many ways, but I continued to express what I wanted and was transparent about what I was doing. That caused a lot of conflict in and of itself, but I would much rather have the true argument about why I'm unhappy because the relationship isn't fulfilling rather than argue about something superficial and continue to live a miserable life. My second spouse wasn't interested in any of my needs or wants and so we ended it, but it was much sooner than it would have been had I still been operating on the old belief that I should avoid conflict and suppress what I want.

Lastly, after practicing your new belief for a while, see the results. Is your life better? Are you more successful with the new belief? Review how effective the new belief is. If things are still not going well, no worries, go through the process again and find out what can be improved. I know that sounds like a lot of work, and it is, but it is worth it and there are no shortcuts unfortunately. You have got to find out what beliefs are holding you back and limiting your growth and replace them with healthy productive beliefs or you will not reach your goals and live the life you want. You deserve better and you can do it. You'll be thrilled when you do.

Review

- We all have limiting beliefs in our lives that hold us back
- We cannot be successful and grow with limiting beliefs
- We must identify the areas that we are unhappy in and find the underlying beliefs we have and evaluate them
- We must change the beliefs that hold us back

Self-Work:

Take some time to look at areas you want to experience more joy or success in. Look at the beliefs you have about those things and then challenge them. It's likely you are holding onto beliefs that are limiting you. Change those beliefs. Embrace new ideas. Write them down. You can use this model:

When it comes to _____
I would like to experience greater satisfaction, success.

I believe these things about myself and the situation:

I would likely be more successful if I believed:

Then try to eliminate the limiting beliefs and replace them with ones that will help you be more successful. Then practice your new belief. See if you have more success as a result of the new belief. After that continue looking for limiting beliefs and going through the same process until you have rooted out many of the mindsets that are holding you back. As always, keep being awesome!

Chapter Four: What do you value?

Work, Work, Work, Work, Work

My father had many areas in which he could have, and even, should have, been better. He was terrible at communicating. He was insensitive. He was stubborn. He often came across cold. He had many virtues as well though and one of the clearest was his work ethic. That man could work. He never seemed to begrudge a task and never seemed short on effort. In retrospect he worked more than anyone else in my life then or now and it is pretty impressive to think about.

My grandfather immigrated to the US from Germany in the early 1950s. He worked and saved and worked some more and eventually started a business with a partner by the 1970s. He worked constantly in what would be called a machine shop, but they did a lot of work creating or repairing plastic injection molds. A "mold maker" is generally what my grandfather and father would say they did. It was difficult work that required precision and tremendous effort as well.

My father worked for my grandfather until we moved as a family from Los Angeles to Fresno, California so my mother could live her dream of being a farmer or a rancher. We ended up on a few acres and began collecting animals.

My father got a job at a plant that, while it changed ownership multiple times, he worked at till he died. But that wasn't the only job he worked. My dad often worked two jobs, not even counting working on the farm with us. He had another job in a manufacturing plant for a while to try to earn enough money for us and the farm, and he even milked cows at a dairy for a while.

I used to go with him halfway across the county, late, so he could milk and feed cows. I helped him, as well as a boy could, and enjoyed those times.

For a long time, my father and I milked all our dairy goats in the morning before he went to work and I to school. We typically milked over 20 does and had as many as 30 in the spring. It was a lot of work and we milked by hand. Somehow, in spite of the fact that I am one of the last people alive who can say he milked goats by hand before going to school, I loved those times.

My father worked. It's what he did. In the end, when he was dying of a brain tumor at 54 years old, he was still talking about how he was going to get a promotion at work. His employer was kind enough to let him come sit in on some meetings while he was sick. It was way too dangerous to let him near machinery, but I appreciated that they were willing to accommodate a dying man, even if his mind was not clear.

My father worked. It's what he loved to do, and I believe it was his top priority. He valued hard work, dedication, loyalty and strength. He embodied all those attributes. While cancer sapped his strength and wilted his once strong body, I still remember him as the strong, stubborn, loyal and dedicated man he was.

In anything however, there are always consequences. My father worked so much that most of my fondest memories of him are when I was working alongside him. Even when he was home, he was often exhausted from working. I don't blame him, I'm just explaining. My father valued work over relationships and over everything else. It makes sense as he was better at working than those other things, but it bothered me that it would only take a call from work and my father was off again, heading in to labor some more. He cursed his work and fretted over it but never quit, never missed a shift and never stopped until his body would no longer let him.

His work was my father's passion and his pride. It is also his legacy, but for me, who wanted more, it left me unsatisfied. I would have rather had more time with him doing other things and I figured I would get that time when he retired but sadly, he never got there, and I never got the time I hoped for. My children didn't get more time with their grandfather, and we are all left wishing we had more of him, but work was more important. It isn't a bad thing, it's just what he valued.

Finding out what you value is of the utmost importance. If you don't know what you value, you may misrepresent yourself to a future partner. If you don't know who you are and what you value, you're far less likely to be involved in the things you truly love.

I knew I wanted kids. I valued family and children, possibly as a result of not having much family and also wanting to redeem my own childhood. Deep, I know. But either way, I knew I wanted children and I wanted to be involved in their lives. I discharged from the army after five years, in spite of the fact that I had had a great career to that point because I knew I didn't want to be deployed and miss that much time with my children; bless those that can. I knew I didn't want that.

I knew I wanted children, and more than one at that. Now, five was more than I anticipated and more than I wanted, but now that they are all here and all peeing in the toilet unassisted, I can say unequivocally that I love all of them and cannot imagine life without them. Being a dad is my favorite thing.

I chose to be a teacher, knowing that the teacher schedule would maximize my time with my children. I now have holidays off with them, including the summer and I am off at the same time each day they are, and I love it. Even divorced and with 50% custody, I get a ton of time with my children. I've coached tons of youth soccer teams and show up at every event possible to cheer them on. They are my world, as cliché as it sounds.

The tradeoff is not making more money. I'm confident that I could absolutely crush it in a different field and was dabbling in finance for a minute but ultimately, a different career would mean different hours and I'm not quite ready to give up my time with my children, especially while they're young.

I'm not upset at all though and I don't run around complaining about my salary or financial situation because I made a choice based on my values to be in a career that supports what I want and that's being with my kids.

Easy right? Well, nothing is easy, but you get the point. We need to figure out what you value so we can structure your life around those things.

Tough Choices

Values are very important for how we operate in almost all aspects of our lives. Whether at work, or with friends or raising kids, the things we value have a major impact on how we interact and how we process events and other people. When we find people who value the same things we do, we tend to feel close to them and when we find people with very different values, we tend to dislike them. In short, our values are foundational to who we are.

That said, often times people cannot articulate clearly what they value, and even if they can, they cannot prioritize those values. Not only is it difficult to know what we value, but it is even more difficult to know which of those values are more important to us because often times values conflict with one another.

For instance, once again, I work in a very diverse community and have identified some values that conflict with one another, but that when push comes to shove, you can figure out which is more important. Here's what I mean. We've probably heard the stereotype that family is very important in Hispanic or Latino cultures. They aren't the only ones of course. Often times family is very important in Italian and Greek families as well. Honestly family is important in every culture otherwise they wouldn't exist. The issue is how important in relation to other values and the Latin culture tends to value it near the top. This has proved true in my classroom as I've seen many students pulled from class for family reasons, often missing weeks of their education. When asked, it is made clear that the priority is family and education can come after that. It isn't to say that cultures who value family don't value education, they do, but they often value family over education.

On the flip side, Asian cultures tend to value education above all else. I served as the advisor to the Asian Club on our campus for many years and they joke all the time about how important grades are in their homes and how even getting B's is sometimes viewed as failure. They joke about "Asian grades" being: A-Average, B-Below Average, C-Can't have dinner, D-Don't come home, F-Find new family. Hilarious! I've had multiple students whose parents went on a trip without them, leaving them with a relative, because the child had school. It is very clear what the value is in those homes; education above all else. Once more, that isn't to say they don't value family, they absolutely do, they just value education more.

Politically and economically this plays out all the time. The most obvious example is with regards to abortion. Don't freak out, I'm the master at dealing with difficult topics, so stay calm and walk through this with me. If you even look at how we talk about it, you can see the conflict of values. Each side is "pro" something. One is pro-choice and the other is pro-life. That doesn't mean that the opposite of pro-choice is anti-choice, even though it seems like it in this instance. It also doesn't mean that the opposite of pro-life is anti-life. I assure you that nearly everyone values choices and also values life. In this debate, however, it comes down to an irreconcilable conflict of values between a woman's right to choose what to do with her own body, and an unborn developing child's right to be born in the first place. It's possibly the most intense conflict of values in our ongoing political debate and there isn't going to be a solution that satisfies everyone. Ever. Respecting that hardly anyone on either side neither hate's woman nor unborn babies, can go a long way in at least lowering the tension between the two sides. But because people hold those values so highly, the debate continues, and the tension continues.

So how are you going to figure out what your values are? It isn't especially easy. Following is a list of common personal values. You really need to identify at least your top ten values. I want you to go through the list and check or write down values that you tend to think are pretty important. In the first round, go ahead and check any that your gut suggests are a big deal. Now, there may be a lot of them because once again, they all tend to be pretty positive and things we may think we want if for no other reason than because others value those things. But you are trying to figure out what you value. So, if it doesn't feel like something that matters all that much to you, don't check it or write it down.

Once you have that initial list, then you need to start going through and prioritizing. What that means is you're going to have to decide which values are more important than others. Maybe you wrote down being content and well as being loyal. Now those are both wonderful things but if you aren't content in your job or in a relationship you may have to leave either in order to be content again but that would mean not being loyal. So, you have to decide whether you value being content more than loyal or whether being loyal worth more than being content. See how quickly this can get difficult?

Keep working on comparing the values you listed until you have a top five. Now, maybe you really can't pick which of your top ten is most important and so on. When that happens it likely means you haven't had to make a difficult choice between your values, but I want you to try anyways. You may find when push comes to shove you will respond differently, but that's ok. As we grow and gain new experiences, we tend to solidify our list. Nothing helps us figure out what really matters to us like losing and being challenged.

Here's the list:

Accomplishment, Success
Accountability
Accuracy
Adventure
All for one & one for all
Beauty
Calm, quietude, peace
Challenge
Change
Cleanliness, orderliness
Collaboration
Commitment
Communication
Community
Competence
Competition
Concern for others
Content over form
Continuous improvement
Cooperation
Coordination
Country, love of (patriotism)
Creativity
Customer satisfaction
Decisiveness
Delight of being, joy
Democracy
Discipline
Discovery
Ease of Use
Efficiency
Equality
Excellence
Fairness
Faith
Family
Family feeling
Flair
Freedom
Friendship
Fun
Global view
Good will
Goodness
Gratitude
Hard work
Harmony
Honesty
Honor
Independence
Inner peace, calm, quietude
Innovation
Integrity
Justice
Knowledge
Leadership
Love, Romance
Loyalty
Maximum utilization (of time, resources)
Meaning
Merit
Money
Openness
Peace, Non-violence
Perfection (e.g. of details)
Personal Growth
Pleasure
Positive attitude
Power
Practicality
Preservation
Privacy
Problem Solving
Progress
Prosperity, Wealth
Punctuality
Quality of work
Regularity
Resourcefulness
Respect for others
Responsiveness
Results-oriented
Rule of Law
Safety
Satisfying others
Security
Self-givingness
Self-reliance
Service (to others, society)
Simplicity
Skill
Speed
Spirit in life (using)
Stability
Standardization
Status
Strength Succeed; A will to- Success, Achievement
Systemization
Teamwork
Timeliness
Tolerance
Tradition
Tranquility
Trust
Truth
Unity
Variety
Wisdom

Did you get your list down to ten values? Were you able to prioritize them? Keep working on it until you can at least get close to accomplishing the task. If you don't know what you value, then you can't actually figure out whether you're living your life authentically and you may run into a lot of problems in your life because other people or things don't line up with the values you don't even know you have. I assure you, as difficult as it is, it's worth it. And remember, just because you leave something off your top ten doesn't mean you don't value it, it just means other values are more important.

What do these values mean?

What did you come up with? I did the exercise myself and I had "personal growth" as my top value which is obvious since I've become obsessed with growing once I realized how much I needed to improve. Next came, communication, then creativity, positive attitude and wisdom. I did a whole list of ten, but this isn't about me. And it was difficult if I'm being honest. There were values I had to leave out of the top ten that seem pretty awesome, but they just weren't as strong as some others.

These values make up your core. These things are the fuel that drive you on a daily basis whether you knew it or not. They were key in most of your decisions. Whenever you made a decision that you were uneasy with, it was probably because it violated one or more of your values. Now that you're aware of them, you can be more mindful about what you're doing and how it will affect other people.

Whenever you are in a situation in which a difficult decision needs to be made, check these values and see which choice more closely reflect what you hold close to your heart. That should reveal the best option for you. Keep in mind, it may not be what others want or what others value but that's because they are operating with a different set of values. You should do what is best for you and what is congruent with your heart and not worry about whether others approve.

When it comes to relationships, especially intimate ones, it is very difficult to maintain harmony and intimacy with someone who doesn't share your values. Believe me. I was with someone who was very narcissistic and selfish, and her values were nothing like mine in the end and there was simply no way we were going to last. Had I had a better grip on what I valued and known these things sooner I could have spared us both a lot of pain. But such is life and that's how we grow.

Still, I recommend having a conversation early in a relationship about values. You can't do that until you know what yours are, but when you've completed this you can compare notes and figure out how compatible you are. There's the secret to relationships success, honestly, you need to be with someone who shares some, not all mind you, but some of your values. Otherwise you will fight all the time and you will likely both be unhappy. I sure as heck was, and so was she. Know yourself and the rest gets easier.

What I'm saying is, you must practice your values. Live them in your life and do not let people put you down for what you value or get you to act in a way contrary to your values. Living counter to our true selves is once again how we end up miserable. Put your values into action in your decision making on a daily basis. Live your authentic life.

Lastly, you may look at the list of values and not actually like some of those things. That's perfectly normal as well. I used to be very competitive, but I didn't actually like myself very much when I was. My competitive value was in conflict with some of my other values like good teamwork and having a positive attitude, so I made a conscious effort to adjust. I began to avoid some, not all, environments that were very competitive, and I began to focus on being positive more than being competitive. I still love to compete, but now when I do, I remember how much I prefer being positive and how much I love personal growth so even if I don't win, I still enjoyed the competition. You can do the same. If there is a value you have that tends to conflict with others that are higher on the list, you can actively work to devalue the problematic one and being a little more congruent. There's no science to it after all, we're talking about your very core so the best you can do is be mindful of how you feel in every situation and try to process through why you feel the way you do.

It isn't going to be easy, but it will be worth it. Every day is another opportunity to live your authentic life and now that you know what you value most in life, you can make choices that align with your heart. Let's get to work.

Review:
- Values are the core of who we are
- We all value different things
- You must identify what you value most and prioritize
- You must check whether your relationships and decisions are congruent with your values

- You can adjust what you value over time if there is a conflict of values
- Living a life that doesn't match your values will make you miserable

Self-Work:

I already described what your work for this lesson is in the earlier section. If you haven't done it yet, you must work on identifying your values. This course is really a ladder or a stairway and if you miss a step the others have less value so make sure you spend time on this. It may actually take a while to really think about because you may need to try to remember times in which you had to make value decisions and that can be difficult. Or you may have to try to imagine different scenarios and then apply values you think you may hold to those situations to get a sense of what you hold closest to your heart.

Another word of caution: often times we adopt our values from our parents as they are our primary models for virtually everything social. As we grow we may find we tend to value other things, so if your first instinct is to say you value Power for example because one or both of your parents are high powered individuals, you may need to see if you actually value that. You may find that you have very different values. That will of course put you at odds with your parents, and believe me, that isn't especially fun, but it is worth the conflict in order to be balanced and at peace with yourself.

Get to work! Figure out what you value so we can continue finding who you are and what you want.

Chapter Five: Being Authentic

Identity Crisis

It may surprise you to know, but I haven't always known who I was and what I wanted. In fact, I lived for many years trying to make other people happy while not paying much attention to who I was. In those years I lost myself. Losing yourself will eventually create an identity crisis. Few things have caused me as much pain as when I was in crisis with myself. You've probably been there too if you're being honest. All teenagers go through this as they try to transition into adulthood from adolescence having just come out of childhood. In fact, there are many transitions to new stages of life that require us to change and it is often uncomfortable to say the least, downright miserable at the worst.

I didn't really know I had lost track of who I was, it happened so slowly and gradually that I couldn't see the change. As I stated earlier, my early 20's, my years in the army were some of the most authentic of my life. I knew who I was, I had values and purpose and goals and everything was going well. I got married at 21 and had to make some compromises, which is fine by the way, then started having kids at 24. I had one then two then three and they kept coming and while I was exhausted and just trying to live day to day, that's when I really began losing myself.

On the outside it looked fine. Wife, kids, church on Sundays and a job; it all appeared to be what many people wanted and maybe in several ways I was an example of what others wanted as well. But I was drained. I had been giving and giving everything I had for everyone else and I didn't know I needed to take care of myself at the same time. It's wonderful to be selfless, much better than being selfish, but I was at risk of running dry and having no more to give.

I felt it. It was small and nagging at first, but I felt myself beginning to fall apart. But so many people had come to rely on me that I didn't want to break. I wanted to stay strong. I wanted to continue to be what I thought everyone wanted me to be. But I knew I couldn't. I couldn't keep up the pace. I needed a break and I needed to rest and I needed to take a moment and evaluate what I wanted and what I needed and who I was.

I really knew something was wrong when I began to have really reckless thoughts. I began to think about abusing drugs and alcohol, something I had never done before, just because the reality of my life was becoming unbearable. I wanted to get in my car and drive away and never come back. I wanted to feel something different than the absolute pain and anguish I was feeling. I wanted to be loved for who I was, but I didn't even know what that was anymore, I just knew that I wasn't content, and I didn't feel right.

I tried to tell people. I expressed my discomfort as articulate as I could, but no one seemed to understand. To be fair, I didn't tell many people, but the ones I did, didn't seem to see that I was falling apart and that I was in crisis. Mostly the message I received back from my attempts to raise alarm were that it would get better and that I should just hold on. But I was barely holding on and I was really afraid I would snap.

But, I did hold on. My wife was pregnant with another child and I decided I would hold on longer for her and for my kids. I held on for more than a year; hurting every single day. At last I couldn't handle it. I nearly lost my daughter, I was losing my dad to a brain tumor, I still wasn't getting my needs met and by then I had no idea what they were any longer. I broke.

For the next year I was in crisis. I was spinning in every direction imaginable. It was absolute chaos. I was grieving, I was hurting, I was searching for meaning and purpose. Nearly everything I thought I knew was called into question. My life was torn down to the foundation; burned to the ground. What's worse is, I lit the fire. I was living so contrary to my authentic self that I couldn't even recognize my life any longer, so I lit it on fire and watched it go up in flames.

In the end I hurt some people along the way, and I have a lot of regrets about that. I finally found myself, however, and figured out why I was hurting so badly. I had gone far too long living for other people and ignore my true self and my own values. It created deep resentment and conflict in me and ultimately, I couldn't recognize myself any longer. It could have been avoided.

Now that you know what your values are, now that you are beginning to get a good sense of who you are, you can live life authentically and avoid an identity crisis like the one I suffered. You can even transition from different stages of life more seamlessly and not endure as much emotional pain and anguish like I did. You can live life in a constant state of confidence and peace knowing who you are and what you value. So, let's focus on embracing that self now.

Your Authentic Self

I hope that by sharing my experience and pain with you, you can understand how dangerous and painful it can be to ignore your authentic self and live life in a manner contrary to your values. I know I'm more than a little dramatic, but I do not want you to endure the suffering that I did when I was living a lie. Few things can feel worse.

So how do you know if you're being authentic? It's easy to know when something is out of whack, honestly. Are you happy? Content? Do you get joy out of life? If not, then what areas are dragging you down?

One of the areas super common for unhappiness is relationships. I don't just mean romantic relationships. You can have a difficult time with family relationships, friends, work colleagues. Maybe your boss is driving you nuts. In any situation, some people are going to be difficult. It's because they don't have the same values that you do. They treat people differently than you and you expect something they are never going to give. It doesn't mean it can never get better and it doesn't mean you have to maintain those relationships. Let's break it down.

If you really have difficulty getting along with someone, it's likely that they value different things than you. Honestly? Some people can't stand me. Difficult to imagine, I know. But I almost never shut up. I will over share, talk about my personal life and express how I feel in almost any situation. I've gotten a little better, but I've been in many staff development meetings and telling myself I should keep my opinion to myself. I rarely do. So, there are some people who don't care for me. It's normal and you should take it personal if someone doesn't like you and if you don't like someone else it also doesn't mean you need to change anything, necessarily. You probably have different values.

So, what should you do when you don't get along with someone? First thing you can do is honestly create some physical distance. I mean literally stay clear of them. There are a couple people I do this with. I decided that there are a few people who aren't even bad people, there's nothing wrong with them, but their values are different from mine, so I get along with them much better if I just limit my interactions with them to pleasantries. Then I even feel like we're friends! It's amazing.

If physical distance isn't enough, then you may consider being clear with them what it is bothers you. I'm hyperverbal so I tend to think talking is a great answer. Now, be prepared for them to be offended because they may feel like you're judging them. You honestly are, but we get a bit too bogged down in this idea that we should never judge anyone or anything. That's silly. We do it all the time. So, if there is something they say or do that is really causing some difficulties between you, then come to them with respect and share that. You may be surprised at how receptive they are. Either way, you verbalized something that is causing you to be unhappy and now there is a chance it gets resolved.

Now, sometimes you do everything with love and respect, and because a person is just not on the same level as you, they decide you're the one with the problem and if you don't like it then that's on you. In a way they're right, you are in fact responsible for how you feel and if they are not interested in respecting that or doing something to make you feel better, then you have to step up your response.

At this point, your options are getting more dramatic. There are two that I recommend that may help. The first is about mourning the person you want them to be and letting go. This is best in intimate relationships like family or romantic partners, although, I actually recommend moving on from a romantic partner if the difference of values is dramatic enough. The strategy is, you look at the person you wish they were, you recognize they are not that person and they will not be that person and you mourn that image is if they actually passed away. I've used this effectively multiple times. There are family members who have just been awful to me consistently. I kept expecting them to be better and value me the way I valued them, but they never changed, and it was causing me tremendous pain. I finally mourned the loss of that image. I let go of my idealized vision of who they could be and who I needed them to be. Then I was able to take them as they were in a realistic and authentic way. This also meant limiting my interactions with them because once I was real about who they were, I no longer had as much desire to be around them.

This happens with parents a lot. As children we idolize our parents. But, as we all know, they are not perfect. Many of them are actually not very healthy and not very good to their own children let alone other people. So rather than hoping that they love you for you and support what you want, it may be time to let go of the idolized version of them and embrace who they really are. This hurts a lot and will challenge everything you believe about them and you, but in the end, you'll be healthier and more authentic.

The other thing you can do is obvious; cut them off. In counseling terms, it is sometimes called going "no contact." That means that you literally no longer answer any form of communication with them and stop spending any time with them. This is best when a person is especially toxic and destructive to you and your mental health. Sadly, there are many toxic people out there. But it doesn't have to be as dramatic as no contact. You may decide you need to end a relationship or stop spending as much time with someone. It doesn't mean you don't answer them when they call or text or whatever, it just means you no longer invest much energy into the relationships. It will save you a ton of emotional energy. You'll be glad you did.

Now, there are plenty of other situations in which your values don't match up. Work can be one for certain. In fact, it's a huge one. I've read surveys that suggest as many as 50% of working people are not happy at their job. It's one of the things I talk to my students about a lot. You ought to go searching for employment that aligns with your values. Your values may change obviously as you grow but you will be much happier and content if you do something that makes you happy every day. I love teaching! It makes me very happy and so I literally gain joy and satisfaction by doing it. That doesn't mean there aren't days that I'm stressed out or frustrated, it just means that I feel good going to work and enjoy what I do.

The work situation can get tricky also. Obviously if you are in a career that is dissatisfying, then try to get into something better suited for your values. If perhaps the environment at your particular work is causing the problem, then try to figure out exactly what it is that is making things difficult and try to enact some changes. Maybe talk to coworkers and see if they experience it like you do and if there are enough people who would like to see some changes then maybe your employer will make them. Happy employees are usually far more productive. I know I am.

Other situations arise as well that may make things difficult for you to be happy and you will have to assess each of them and see if they can be improved. Maybe you simply hate the area you live in. Can you move? Is your home making you unhappy? Perhaps you can find a different one. Or maybe you a spending your leisure time doing things that are not congruent with your values. Maybe your circle of friends is bringing you down. It may be time for a change. Perhaps you need a new activity that brings you joy. The world is an amazing and wonderful place and there are endless opportunities out there that can and will bring you joy. Work on finding them. You'll be glad you did.

Review

- Living in a way that isn't incongruent with your values will make you unhappy
- Doing so for extended periods of time may lead to an identity crisis
- You are living in a way counter to your values if you experience consistent unhappiness
- There are many ways to address your unhappiness and live your authentic life

Self-Work:

Take some time to examine what areas of your life bring you joy and which ones bring you down. You can literally make a list. In education we sometimes call this a "graphic organizer" or a "T" chart. Put a line down the center of your page. Title one side "joy" and the other "pain" or one "positive" and the other "negative." It doesn't really matter what you label the sides, the point is, you are going to list areas of your life that are going well and others that are a struggle. If you're the type of person that has difficulty choosing from only two options, then maybe create a middle column that is neutral. If you're a very deep thinker, perhaps you even need to turn a page and create a spectrum of zero to ten with zero being no joy and ten being the most joy and plot your life on the spectrum to get a sense of the areas that are going well and others that need improvement.

It doesn't much matter how you go about examining your life, the point is you need to do so. Once you have listed areas of your life, you can then examine both sides. Begin with the positives. What about those areas makes you happy? What is it that brings you joy? Can you identify why? It's likely that those areas are well aligned with your values that we identified in the previous section. Then look at the list of aspects of your life that are bringing you down. What about those areas is difficult? Is the people? Is it the environment? Try to see, once again, if there is a conflict of values that is causing you distress. Even take it a step further and see if there is one area that is worse than the others. Perhaps there is one part of your life that is really bringing you down and if you could improve it you would be much healthier and happier. If you can then we can focus on making that change immediately and you'll be a much better version of you right away.

It isn't going to be easy but do the work. Examine your life and find out which areas are authentic to who you are and which ones are not.

Chapter Six: What are your Dreams?

Disney's Dream

Let's mix it up. I've been sharing plenty of stories of my own experience but for this chapter, I feel the story of Walt Disney is much better suited to make the point about dreams. Besides, everyone loves Disney.

Walt Disney is known around the world, and he honestly knew he wanted to be an animator from a very early age. He was drawing a ton by the time he was in high school and he was animating cartoons for his school newspaper by then as well. He even took classes in drawing as a teen. It appeared he was well on his way to living his dream. But then World War I, the Great War, dragged the United States into its deadly midst.

Walt Disney quit school to try to enlist in the military at 16 but was rejected for being too young and instead served in the Red Cross. He came home in

1919 and got a job drawing cartoons for a newspaper and began experimenting with film and creating his own cartoons in motion picture.

Within a couple years, Walt Disney opened his first studio. He even began hiring employees and making his own animated films. Sadly, he went bankrupt by 1923 and had to close his first studio. By all accounts he was in absolute financial ruin at that point. But Walt Disney didn't give up on his dream of creating a fantastic animation studio.

Walt pooled his money with his brother and another animator, and they moved to Los Angeles and created a new studio. They landed a distribution contract to make shorts with a few characters they developed. The distributor completely screwed over the studio and stole the rights to their work along with all their animators. Another blow that might have ended Walt's dream.

The three original founders of the studio remained and together, with their wives, they managed to produce some new animated films. The one that really took off was the now famed, "Steamboat Willie" which featured the character we now know as Mickey Mouse. It was a huge success. They then created some more shorts and their film of the Three

Little Pigs became the most popular movie during the Great Depression.

The studio produced Snow White and the Seven Dwarves and the movie grossed more than an amazing million dollars and won eight academy awards. That was during the Great Depression. His dream was becoming reality in spite of the worst economic conditions the nation had ever experienced.

All was not smooth sailing from there however, and in 1941, there was an animator's strike during which many of their employees resigned and the company took years to recover from the set back.

In 1955 the company opened their theme park but even that had many setbacks, including a number of counterfeit invitations being sent out causing massive confusion and resentment. The project cost $17 million.

There were plenty of other setbacks along the way that often resulted in Walt Disney suffering depression and anxiety along with fits of rage.

MGM actually told Walt that his Mickey Mouse idea would never work because the giant mouse on the screen was too scary, especially to women. Oops, Mickey is one of the most recognizable characters of all time.

There was a lot of resistance to the release of the Three Little Pigs because the film only contained the three pigs and the wolf, and it was thought there weren't enough characters to keep people interested. Wrong again.

When they premiered Snow White and the Seven Dwarves for a group of college students, Walt was really upset when they left half way through the film. He assumed they didn't like it, but it later turned out that the students had a curfew and had to leave for their dorms.

Pinocchio almost never happened because the film was over budget and Walt decided to make some significant changes to it along the way. The studio lost a million dollars on the film in its first release. Only later was it popular and grossed income.

Some thought that it was a fantastic idea to hire a bunch of little people to sit on top of the theater when Pinocchio was released and greet people when they arrive to view the film. They apparently gave the group a bunch of food and wine to keep them satisfied during the long day. Eventually it resulted in a group of drunk and then naked little people on top of the building who had to be arrested by the police. Bad move.

Fantasia bombed and Disney never lived to see it successful. It turns out releasing Bambi in which the fawn's mother is shot in the opening scene during the midst of World War Two wasn't clever either. Song of the South? Ouch.

We won't even go there, it's far too racist to even talk about now.

Today the company is worth more than $100 billion. It employs more than 166,000 people. Disney is a worldwide brand and Walt has a legacy that cannot be easily matched.

The point is, it all began with a boy who loved to draw and had a dream and in spite of many difficulties, in spite of being so broke at one point he apparently ate dog food to stay alive, in spite of people actively trying to ruin him, he endured and maintained his dream and now he is immortal.

Dreams are important. Maybe few people have the courage to dream, or maybe we decide that they will never be achieved, but I say they can. Many have achieved their dreams and even far more than they ever dreamed possible and you can too. Your dreams matter, let's talk about them and how we can make them a reality.

Dream Vs. Fantasy

First thing first, we need to be clear what constitutes a dream. Sometimes people are running around complaining that their dreams don't come true and when you ask them about their dreams, they really aren't dreams at all; they're fantasies. I work with over 200 teenagers every year and they have plenty of dreams but also sometimes live in absolute fantasy.

I, just this last week, had to have a discussion with a young man who is failing every single class. I was trying to find a way to motivate him and get him to realize that he just isn't really on a path that is going to get him anywhere. I pointed out that if he spent another semester failing then he is pretty much guaranteed to not finish high school. He's a junior and it isn't going well for him. So, I tried to point out that not finishing high school will make it very difficult for him to find a job. He wasn't fazed. He said he could just sell drugs. Of course. Because that's a fantastic life plan. He tried to counter with the fact that Jay-Z sold drugs. This kid is no Jay-Z. I tried to counter by pointing out that Jay-Z is actually very industrious and works very hard and that this kid doesn't even bush his own hair and that selling drugs is just going to land him in jail. Nope, kid is set on failing all his courses and eventually (if he isn't already) selling drugs. That is not a dream, that's a fantasy in which you can be completely irresponsible and unproductive and somehow still have things you want.

Dreams are reasonable and dreams are achievable. It's ok to dream big by the way as long as you can develop a plan to make those dreams a reality.

I had a dream to play professional baseball after I hit my one and only homerun as a kid. Now, I didn't have a plan to achieve that dream and I didn't put in much energy to get to that dream either, and coupled with my very average natural physical talent, that dream never happened. But had I supported that dream, maybe I could have had more success with baseball.

Is it your dream to just marry someone rich and drink martini's all day? That's nice. How are you going to pull that off? Believe it or not, there aren't a ton of wealthy people running around looking for someone to sit around in their home and drink their alcohol while being entirely unproductive. So maybe that's a little more of a fantasy too.

Your dream needs the elements we just mentioned. It needs to be something you can actually achieve. That doesn't even mean it has to be something that other people achieved. There are plenty of dreams that were the first ones. The first person in space, the first African American president, the first person to run a mile under four minutes, there are plenty of things that no one has done before that are probably achievable. Elon Musk wants to go to Mars and colonize other planets. Sounds weird to me because I like this planet, but it's his dream and I'm confident he can pull it off.

Besides being achievable, your dreams need to be things that can be something you can work and build towards. I can hardly imagine a dream in which you can simply wake up one day and nail it on the first try. If that's the case then maybe you don't have a dream, you have a task you haven't tried before. Your dreams ought to be things that will take some time and sustained effort to reach.

Your dreams need to be things that align with your values. I want to get a house by a lake near me for me and my kids to enjoy. It's a bit of a dream because it has those other elements, but it is also something that matches the things I value most. If your dream doesn't match your values, then you probably won't even enjoy it and perhaps it isn't actually your dream but someone else's. Do you really want to be a doctor? Or is that a dream your parents have for you? Do you really want to have children? Or is that a dream your spouse has. Be real about what you value and whether your dreams match them. Now that you know what constitutes a dream, it's time to look at them.

What are your Dreams?

Now it's time to get real with yourself. Do you have any dreams, or did you let the weight and disappointment of life steal them from you? Don't be ashamed, plenty of people lose sight of their dreams and get bogged down with daily life. You can make new ones though. Let's dream again.

First of all, if you have dreams still, let's look at them. Write them down. What are they? Do they have the elements we discussed in the last section? Maybe you even need to look at them and make sure you still want those dreams. Chances are, if you came up with them a long time ago, you don't even want those dreams any longer. That's entirely ok, mind you. We grow, we change, we have different needs and different dreams. So, check to see if you have solid dreams.

If you don't have any dreams then it's time to make some. They don't have to be outrageous and they for sure don't have to be something other people dream about. Is your dream to retire early in a small cabin? Sounds awesome! Maybe you dream of traveling across Europe one day? Or visiting the nation your ancestors were from? Maybe you want to own a really nice vehicle that you've always admired, or maybe you want to compete in a marathon. There are a ton of dreams that require time and commitment that may not be things other people dream about but that mean something to you.

They may even be relationship dreams. Honestly? After two failed marriages, I still dream of having a completely amazing supportive mutually loving relationship. Maybe you dream of having a bunch of children and all the nights watching a movie together snuggled up on the couch. Dreams come in many shapes and sizes and they only need to mean something to you.

Once you have your dreams you need to commit them to writing. Maybe you want to save them on your phone so you can see them every day. Or maybe you want to write them down and put them on the fridge. Or put them by your nightstand so you can look at them when you go to sleep and wake up. Some people tape them to the mirror in the bathroom so they can keep them in their mind constantly. The point is, you need to keep your dreams in your mind regularly or you'll lose sight of them and forget that you once had dreams. If you don't know where you want to be in your dreams, then you'll never get there.

Dream big and hold on to them. Lastly, make a plan to get there. Will it take money? Start saving. Do your dreams require someone else? Then begin looking for the person to share that dream with. Figure out which steps you need to take to get there and begin taking them. Even just one small step means you're a little closer to that dream. You deserve to live your dreams. Love yourself enough to pursue them.

Review
- Dreams are an important part of enjoying our lives
- Dreams are very different from fantasies
- Dreams are achievable
- Dreams take consistent work and effort
- Your dreams need to align with your values
- Write your dreams down so they are ever in your heart and on your mind

Self-Work:

I already mentioned it but let me make it clear. You need to make a list of your dreams. You also need to write some details about these dreams. The more the better. The more energy you commit to casting these dreams the more real they will become. Do you want to travel to Europe? When? Where exactly? Who is going to be with you? Do you want to backpack or drive or cruise down rivers? Look into it and do some research about the details of your dream. The more details you can apply to it the better.

Make multiple dreams. Do not just stop at one. Come up with a few of them. You may not get to live all of them, but you need to go for them anyways. This way you can adjust as you grow and life changes.

Lastly, take a moment to write a few sentences about why each of those dreams align with your values. It is so important that everything we do, every decision we make, is true to who we are, that you must make sure your dreams all also true to you. They must also be authentic and real.

To recap, come up with a list of dreams that you already have or that you thought up now, Add as many details as you can to your dreams. The more the better. Then explain how those dreams are in alignment with your values. How are they true to who you are? Next, we'll work on making those dreams real!

Chapter Seven: Setting Goals

Belts and Ranks

We talk about how important goals are all the time. We even tend to set a new goal or resolution every new year that would make our lives better, and yet well over 90% of people who make a resolution are not keeping it after the first month. That's pretty weak.

Indeed, goals are important and yet, as a whole, we are really pathetic at keeping them and achieving them. That has got to stop if we're going to be our best selves. It's time to reach our goals.

Perhaps what we really need is some shaming. I know, it's the 21st century and we are all about protecting people's feelings. I don't mean that we actively shame people, but it is possible to shame people without drawing any attention to the fact that they are lame.

As I've made clear already, I was in the army. I left immediately out of high school and served for five years. You probably also know, but if you don't let me tell you, in the military, rank is made very clear. In fact, every soldier, marine, airman and sailor wear his or her rank with every uniform. In the army the lowest of all ranks is the private. A private actually has no visible rank. Your collar, headgear and every bit of your uniform is bare. It's pretty weak. But most everyone begins there so there is no shame in it when you've only just begun serving. Most everyone advances to the second rank, Private Second Class, at the end of six months of service. Then on to Private First Class, then Corporal or Specialist and then to Sergeant. So on and so forth.

The rank system is brilliant. It lets a person know immediately what level of achievement a person has, and you can give them the appropriate level of respect. Officers are all to be saluted and if one were to enter a room it was protocol to call the room to attention.

For me, I set a goal to make sergeant, (enlisted rank 5) before I discharged at the end of five years. There was a lot to do in order to achieve the rank including an interview panel, physical test, marksmanship test and a course I had to complete. I was set on making that rank however and worked hard to achieve it. I even found I could take a test to try to gain college credit. They were called CLEP tests or "college level examination program" and being a somewhat clever guy, I managed to take and pass a number of them in order to gain some more promotion points.

I managed to make sergeant and I was very proud when I did. Even now when I talk to current soldiers or service members or prior ones, when they ask what rank I achieved in my five years, I'm very proud to say I made sergeant and I feel I receive a little more respect as a result. After all, sergeant is a rank in the "non-commissioned" officer category and represents a decent level of achievement.

If only life had ranks. How awesome would it be if we wore our achievements around all day? Would you make more goals and keep them? I certainly would. I would be ashamed to be the guy walking around with no achievements or a low rank. Those people existed in the army as well.

There were plenty of people who had been in the military for a number of years who had not achieved much and so their rank was lower than their peers who had been serving a similar length of time. There were also soldiers who had rank removed from them because of discipline issues. That too reflected poorly on them. I feel it motivated everyone to be more productive, set more goals and work towards achieving those goals.

A comparable system is the belt system in martial arts. Apparently, the system is only about 150 years old, but it is a system in which you can tell a person's achievement merely by the color of their belt. Similar to the military, respect is given to the higher ranks as their belt signifies a level of mastery higher than others. It's brilliant. We should all run around with belts on in life!

Since we are not likely going to create a system in which our achievements and levels are made plain to everyone in regular life, we are going to have to hold ourselves accountable. I assure you, if you haven't learned yet, achieving your goals and growing will lead to increased joy and contentment. If you're not doing so already, it's time to set goals and reach them.

What Goals Should You Set?

Maybe part of the problem is that we don't really know what goals we ought to set. In the previous section I cited the military and martial arts as an example of systems with goals but those are obvious. Life doesn't have a series of belts or ranks with predefined criteria for reaching those goals. But that's also the advantage. We get to set our own goals and achieve our own levels of success.

So then what goals should you set? Let's keep using the same strategy. What areas of your life are you dissatisfied with? Are you unhappy at work? Then let's make some career goals. Are you unhappy in a relationship? Then it's time to make some goals related to that. Or maybe you're unhappy with your health, your home, your knowledge and wisdom. Figure out which areas of your life you want to improve, then improve those areas.

Be real with yourself. We've talked about it already, but we are too good at protecting our own ego. I've been there. I've for sure rationalized some nonsense that I was doing and pretending like it wasn't having a negative impact on my life and that I was fine with it. You must look at yourself and be honest about where you can be better. Write those things down. Where are you not good enough. We all have areas where we need to get better. Even people at the top of their game stay there because they are constantly looking for areas where they could get better.

Not sure where those things are? Well where are you failing? That's exactly where you need to start. Failure is the best teacher for where we need to grow. Two divorces in five years made it abundantly clear to me that I needed to drastically improve in that area. If I had any hope of having a healthy relationship at any point, I was going to need to find out what I was doing that was contributing to poor relationships. I began to look at all my behaviors and decisions and I found the things I needed to do better. I studied, I watched hours of lectures and talks on YouTube and I learned. Point is, you can easily find the areas where you need to grow; if you're honest.

I like to look at our existence in the three main categories: mind, body and spirit. When it comes to spirit, I usually explain that the spirit is our emotional life. There's a fourth area that can be a focus for growth is our social and relationship life, but the internal three are the ones most in our control so we should focus there first and then the social will usually improve.

Body is the most straight forward. I'm not a doctor, obviously, and I'm not a nutritionist, but if we are not healthy physically then the others (mind and spirit) suffer. Don't think so? I've watched students sit in class with only a couple hours of sleep because they were up all night entertaining themselves and then stuffing their face with hot Cheetos and they were unable to focus their attention and learn effectively. Have you ever overeaten to the point where you felt sick? Was your mind especially clear? Were you emotionally balanced?

There are a lot of things we do that are not great for our bodies and that's really sad because our bodies are actually fantastic at keeping us going and healthy. Our bodies literally filter poisons out to keep us healthy, yet we dump more poison in.

We all widely accept that smoking is bad for us, yet plenty of people are still smoking. And some that will quickly point out how unhealthy smoking is, have no problem dumping tons of refined sugar into their bodies on a daily basis. What about alcohol? Is that healthy for your body? I've seen an increase in teenagers with joint and muscle issues. Why? Maybe they are not exercising enough, if at all. Not to throw the school system under the bus, but students mostly walk around or even sit during physical education now and it isn't the teachers' fault. I assure you the P.E. teachers are very much into health and exercise. No, it's the public education system that has made it so easy to succeed in P.E. that it takes virtually no effort at all.

If you don't feel well, chances are, something is not going well with your body. Figure out what it is and set yourself some goals. Consult a doctor or talk to a health professional. Eat more vegetables and fruits. Cut out sodas and fast food from your diet. Begin exercising more. Do something! But set yourself a goal and make it happen. Your mental and emotional states are directly connected to your physical health. Hence the adage, "if you haven't got your health, you haven't got anything."

Now the mind aspect of the personal trinity is simple. Are you learning anything? When's the last time you read something? Had a discussion about something new? Took a class? Watched a documentary? Some of us are by nature, curious. I'm one of those. I never get tired of learning. I can't get enough of it honestly. I would love to be in a formal learning environment all the time, and in fact I am as a teacher. But even as a teacher I never get tired of learning new things about the subjects I teach.

Now, I get that there are many people out there who are not, what I like to call, academic. That doesn't mean you shouldn't be learning something new. You must be into something. You must have some area of interest or some hobby. You can become an expert in whatever it is you're into, but the point is, be into something and keep learning. If we don't then our minds get a bit stagnant and our thoughts and insights become very predictable and routine. There is plenty of evidence out there to suggest that when we do not push our minds, they begin to weaken a bit just like muscles and when we exercise them they grow stronger.

Our mind is also very powerful to control the other aspects of our being. There is literally a whole study now generally referred to as, "mindfulness," of which I'm a bit of a student. I even hope to be a master of it soon so that I can teach others how to use the power of their minds to affect other aspects of their being. The power of our minds is such that hypnosis and suggestion are very strong forces. It's been reported that operations have been performed without anesthesia but without pain as a result of hypnosis and suggestion. If you do not have a strong mind, then you cannot use it to benefit your body and spirit, but if you exercise it, you can achieve powerful things. So, it's time to set some goals to learn some new things and strengthen your mind.

Lastly, and probably this is the one everyone can and should set some goals on, spirit. And again, I use the word spirit to describe our emotional state. Many people connect spirit with the religious experience and practice and that's entirely fine. Indeed, religious practice is very spiritual.

So many people in the developed world battle with some level of depression and anxiety. Many have issues with anger or rage. Others tend to suffer from fears. Virtually every person could be happier and healthier if they were better able to manage their emotional state.

Again, our spiritual or emotional health has a tremendous impact on the other two; mind and body. When we are upset we cannot think especially clearly. When we are angry or afraid or sad our emotions tend to override our minds and control our decisions. Most everyone is familiar with the emotional state of "fight or flight," and sometimes psychologists add "freeze" as one of the responses as well. It is an emotional state brought on by some sort of danger or threat and it hijacks our thinking to make us very reactionary. We do that because our emotional self is trying to preserve our being and is taking over so protect us. However, our spirit is only interested in our survival in those moments and so it doesn't often make the best choice.

Have you even been very stressed out? I have. Stress has a massive impact on our physical health besides our reasoning ability. People often experience unhealthy weight loss or weight gain as a result of stress. Many report hair loss or other physical symptoms. I know my stomach will often hurt when I am stressed out, other get bad headaches. Our emotional health has a huge influence on the rest of our being. What areas do you feel you can improve? Set some goals to improve your emotional state and stick to them.

Lastly, once we've addressed areas in which we can improve internally, we can begin to look at external things we might set some goals for. We already mentioned some of these, but they might be career, financial or relationship goals. No matter where you are in life, there are probably some things that can be improved. Keep in mind though that your changes should begin with you because you can certainly control you much easier than you can control your job or other people. So, work on you for certain by setting some goals and then also set some external goals you would love to see reached.

How do you set goals?

Goal setting is fairly easy if you follow a well-accepted acronym "SMART." Keeping your goals is another story. I highly recommend using this method for setting appropriate goals and doing so will set you up for success and you'll meet more of your goals.

The S stands for "specific." This means you cannot have something like "be healthier," or "learn things." You must be more specific about how you want to healthier or what you want to learn. So, you could set a goal to "lose 30 pounds," or "read a book every month." Now we actually have a specific goal that we can reach for. Do this in all areas that you think you may need to improve and keep in mind you can brainstorm many goals then select a few to focus on so you are not overwhelmed.

Next is "measurable." This means we need to be able to have a way to measure whether you're meeting your goal or not. In the example of weight it is easy and with regards to reading books it is as well. But you can create a measurable standard with almost anything if you think about it. Maybe you want to increase your income by 10%. We for certain can verify whether you met that goal. Or if it is a spiritual goal, then you can say, you want to limit the days you feel depressed to no more than twice a month or something like that. Don't get twisted thinking you can't limit the days you feel depressed. Unless you are medically depressed, we can all manage our emotional states and pull ourselves out of a depression.

The third aspect of SMART goals is "achievable." This means you are making sure that your goal is something you can actually make a reality. If you're only making $30,000 and you want to make $100,000 by the end of the year then you better have a really good plan to get there, otherwise it isn't an especially achievable goal. Don't be afraid to lower your expectations to the point where your goal is finally achievable. In fact, I recommend, especially when working on an area in which you've typically had poor success, starting off with a very modest goal. One you achieve your modest goals then you can step them up and work towards something more difficult. When we achieve some of the easier goals, we will build momentum and motivation as well to continue to grow and improve.

Next is "reasonable." Now, I feel like the developers of this system really wanted to make the acronym spell "SMART," so they decided to force it and put "reasonable" after "achievable." In my mind they are super similar. However, let's consider reasonable to mean something that will actually make a difference in your life. Is it reasonable to want to lose weight? Of course it is! Is it reasonable to set a goal to eat 10 cheeseburgers in one sitting? No! That's a ridiculous goal. So, for the purposes of goal setting, let's allow reasonable to mean something that is going to improve your life. It's reasonable to want to improve relationships, but it isn't a reasonable goal to say you want to get more tattoos. You're free to do that with no judgment but it isn't a reasonable life goal as it doesn't necessarily add to the value of your life. And yes, I know there are tattoo people out there who are going to disagree with me and that's perfectly fine. I'm more interested in helping people improve their habits, mindset and levels of success than how awesome their ink is. That said, I definitely want some tattoos.

The final aspect of smart goals is "time." You need to give yourself a timeframe to complete these goals. If it's weight, how long are you giving yourself to drop it? If it's about learning, then when do you need to have this goal completed by? Putting a timeframe on your goals helps to keep you accountable to them. It helps you to make sure you stay focused on achieving them.

In summary, I highly recommend that you go through this process and set several goals for yourself. Once you've done that, just like we did with our dreams, you need to keep them somewhere obvious so you can see them daily and keep your mind focused on those goals. Believe me, once you begin to reach some of these goals it is going to become addicting. You'll be able to measure the actual growth in your life and it will feel fantastic. I'm excited about how much you're going to achieve by using SMART goals!

Review
- In life we are not great at marking our achievements and keeping track of our goals
- Goals are essential to improving in areas of our life in which we could be more successful
- We all have areas that can be improved, look for areas in which you have experienced some failure or disappointment for clues
- Be aware that we are Mind, Body and Spirit and that failure in any of

them can lead to decreased success in the others
- Using the SMART Goal model for goal setting will help us to achieve our goals

Self-Work:

I've already essentially laid out the self-work for this section but let's make sure we put it all together. You need to make some goals for yourself. I suggest looking at areas of your life that you would like to improve and beginning there. If you have trouble figuring out the areas that you ought to improve, think about the areas in which you haven't been as successful as you would like. Once you find those you can find appropriate goals.

Besides working on areas in which you could have greater success, I also recommend setting at least one goal for each aspect of being: mind, body and spirit. We can all improve all the time and the most successful people never stop improving, it's why they're the best. Think about yourself and come up with at least one goal for each.

Write your goals down! I even recommend putting them into categories: mind, body, spirit, career, social, family or whatever. That way you can also track where you're growing and where you are not.

Use the SMART acronym to give your goals some details. Even write it all out with the goals when you're putting them all together.

Lastly, place your goals somewhere that you can see them daily. I recommend putting them near your dreams as well. That way you can have them on your mind always. If they are on our minds we can stay focused on them better. Whatever it is you need to remind yourself of your goals and stay moving towards achieving them. Get to work, you're well on your way to being amazing.

Chapter Eight: Patterns for Success

Marky Mark

Now that you've done a ton of work on yourself, you've looked at who you are and who you want to be, then committed to your dreams and goals and decided to live by your values and your authentic life, the hard part begins. Now you need to live your life in full awesomeness. It's easier said than done. What it takes is discipline.

Here's a fact: highly successful and productive people are also highly disciplined and have good habits. Whether they are athletes, or business men or entertainers, the most successful people are often very focused and very disciplined, and they develop habits that support their excellence.

Recently, Mark Wahlberg shared his schedule on Instagram and we were all shocked at what a machine the man is. If you're not familiar, Mark Wahlberg was a singer and performer early in his life, performing as Marky Mark and the Funky Bunch. "Good Vibrations" was probably his biggest hit and he was never a massive star in that right, but was respectable and had a few tracks that made the charts. He then got into acting. He stared in more than a few movies and lately continues look fantastic and be featured in films. He has a solid career and is involved in a variety of ventures. He is worth $255 million. He isn't even 50 yet. Yeah, he's pretty successful. He's also shockingly attractive, which helps but that takes work as well. His body doesn't stay that fit accidentally.

According to Marky Mark himself, he wakes up before 3 AM and prays, then eats, works out, eats, works out, showers then plays golf at like 7:30 AM. So, he's already done two workouts before many of us even wake up. His body is fantastic though. The rest of his day is highly structured as well and includes constant working out and snacking while also getting some business done, spending time with his family and eventually he goes to sleep at 7 PM. The man is a machine.

Oh, you think Kevin Hart doesn't work hard? Please. The man's motto is literally "Everyone wants to be famous, no one wants to do the work." He works a ton and is very structured in his time.

I listened to Elon Musk interview with Joe Rogan and how that man gets done all the things he does in a day blows my mind.

I read that President Teddy Roosevelt read a book a day. President George Bush had a reading competition with his staff and won. The younger president Bush also realized that drinking wasn't doing him any good and he replaced it with running, and at 60 years old the man was still running a 20 minute 3 mile. He would have dusted me in a race and I'm much younger.

Justin Bieber may be talented but he spends a lot of time partying and hasn't put an album out since 2015 and has put out 4 albums in total. Meanwhile, although he's obviously much older, Paul McCartney is more than 70 years old but had an album out as recently as 2018 and already has a single out in 2019. He's a highly disciplined structured artist and in his lifetime he's recorded 25 solo studio albums (not the Beatles) 7 live albums and multiple other compilation albums, EPs and others. He's prolific. He's disciplined.

These highly successful people never stop. They have fantastic habits that support their success and they are taking care of their minds, bodies and spirits. You have got to find a way to incorporate good habits into your life if you would like to be successful. Now, that doesn't mean you need to be as productive as some of these people, but you have got to be committed to your dreams and goals and have got to organize your life in a way that supports them. If you do not, then you will not ever be the best version of yourself and you deserve to be that person. Believe that.

Useful Habits and Mindsets

We cannot be truly successful, nor can we be our best versions of ourselves if we have poor habits and mindsets. It really can be that easy. Two people can experience the exact same event and have completely different reactions based on their differing mindsets. And two people can have very similar backgrounds and natural talents and abilities but with different habits can have very different levels of achievement and success. Having the discipline to live your authentic life is crucial in actually doing so. That said, let's look at some habits and mindsets that will help you reach your full potential.

One that is huge can be described in several ways, but it boils down to being a master of your reality. It seems cosmic or mystical sometimes, but we really do experience the world through our own reality. I read book about how powerful our minds are and one of the examples it gave was how people register gunshot wounds as far as pain is concerned. In hospitals in the civilian world, gunshot patients tend to register their pain level at a 9 or 10. The military found that soldiers who had a gunshot wound that wasn't life threatening tended to register the pain at a 5 or 6. The difference wasn't that the soldiers were just that much tougher than everyone else, but the fact that the gun shot meant they got to go home. They got to leave a dangerous war and return to the safety of their home and family. That pain brought with it a ticket home and away from a warzone. So, if your brain can literally register the pain of a wound differently, you can absolutely manage how you perceive the world. It isn't just about being optimistic, because it's important to be realistic, but it's about looking forward to the next opportunity rather than fixating on missed ones in the past. There is always something great available to you, master your reality and shape it to suit your needs and create your joy.

    Another thing that is very useful is embracing change. Things will change. You cannot expect to stay in one place and do the exact same thing every day and get the same result. And guess what? Change can hurt. It makes us uncomfortable. Change causes us stress, but it doesn't have to. Just like you can shape your own reality, you can embrace change. Rather than looking at change as a problem. When you understand that change is normal and natural you can begin to anticipate those changes and not let them get you down but rather, you can even be excited about them because you know you have a chance to do something new and grow.

For one last mindset that I feel you should embrace, how about don't complain? I feel like far too many people complain rather than face issues head on and just resolve them. There will always be something to complain about, just like there will always be something to celebrate. Be the person who take adversity and uses it to grow rather than sitting around and complaining. It never solves anything, and it doesn't help you grow at all. Furthermore, if you surround yourself with other people who complain, then you will all be miserable and likely not grow at all. Instead, take each day and each event as it comes and use it as an opportunity to build, to grow and to improve. Embrace a growth mindset and ditch the complaining.

Now for some helpful habits. First and foremost, give yourself a wake up time. I mean a set time to get up and begin your day. Your brain loves patterns and predictability. Give yourself a set time to get up, preferably a time that allows you room to focus on yourself, to set up your day for success and to do some things that help you be better. You might get up and exercise or pray or meditate or read. Perhaps it will do you good to cook breakfast or even make breakfast for your family. Whatever it is, make sure you give yourself time in the morning, otherwise you'll be rushed and late and it will ruin your ability to be productive and joyful.

Another important habit is to get yourself on some sort of diet. I don't mean for losing weight necessarily, I just mean eating regular and planned meals. When we wake in the morning our bodies are a bit of a mess. We're dehydrated so you should certainly drink water and we're also hypoglycemic because our bodies haven't had any food to process. I read that if our bodies do not get food to eat in the morning and we cannot get out of hypoglycemic mode, it literally effects our ability to think the remainder of the day as our brains are stuck in a survival mode. There are other eating habits that are poor for us as well, but the point is, our bodies do better when our diet is more regular and predictable so pay attention to the fuel you're putting in your machine. If you put poor fuel in, or you let the tank run empty, we don't function as well.

I highly recommend you also schedule time to do something you're passionate about. Maybe it's your hobby or maybe, like me, you have a side gig that you enjoy. Whatever it is, make sure you're giving yourself time for it so that you can be stimulated. Even better, set aside scheduled time to focus on your dreams and goals. That way you'll constantly be mindful of them and you'll also be working your way towards them every day or week.

There are other options for things you can include in your daily structured schedule. You might include exercise as part of your daily routine which will help your emotional state and mental focus. Maybe you want to do yoga as a way to increase flexibility and manage stress. Family time ought to be included so make sure there is time for that as well. Remind yourself what your values, goals and dreams are and commit to some daily habits that will support them. Otherwise you're not living your authentic life.

How to Form Good Habits

The first tip I have is to sit down and write out what your ideal day would look like. Seriously, write down your full schedule and look at it. Too few of us do this but then we're quick to complain that we don't have any time. Make sure you list your priorities, as in the things you really want to accomplish in a normal day. That way you'll already be aware of whether there is even time for all the things you want to do. If something really important to you didn't make the schedule, then you may need to reprioritize. Try to align your schedule as closely as you can with your values.

After a daily schedule, come up with things you want to save time for every week. It may not be possible after all to do everything you want every day or even every work day, so come up with some things that are important but that you can't accomplish every day. List which day you will assign to those tasks. Maybe you really enjoy golf so you want to do it every Saturday. Maybe you love getting coffee with your friends, but they can't get together every day so it's a Sunday afternoon task. You get the idea.

With these two lists, you can even come up with a schedule for an entire week. That way you can see how often you participate in everything and you can further analyze whether you are doing the things you really love and value enough, or whether you are wasting a lot of time with things that don't add to your life or help you grow. Be real with yourself and try to look objectively at your week.

Now comes the more difficult part, creating healthy habits. I'm not going to lie, it isn't going to be easy at first. Your body will want what it's used to and if it's used to poor habits then it will want to stay lazy and wasteful. It's going to be a painful process at first, but it will be worth it.

You have to start with the first things on your daily schedule and that's the time you wake up. You've absolutely got to wake up when you said you would. It may not feel good at first. Work on changing your mindset about it. It may seem silly, but go to bed thinking about how good you are going to feel getting up when you schedule it. Tell yourself how happy you are going to be when you are getting more done and being more productive. Think about the task you scheduled for yourself first thing in the morning. Make it a task you really enjoy and that makes you feel good. That way you have a good reason to get up when you do. It's even better if the task feeds your mind, body or spirit. Feel better when you work out? Then do that first thing and remind yourself often how good you will feel after you work out. Enjoy reading? Do that first thing. Maybe a cooked meal and some tea or coffee sets your day right. Read some scriptures or motivating book and get your mind in the right place. No matter what task you choose for yourself first thing, make sure it makes you feel good and gets your day off to a good start.

It takes about two months to develop a strong habit. It is often helpful to cue your brain by creating something to associate your new behavior with. It could be an object, a sound or music, or even the clothes you choose. When I'm teaching, I have my lanyard with my keys on it forever in my pocket or near me. I tend to fiddle with it while I'm in my teaching zone. The lanyard literally primes my brain to get me into the right mental state to teach. I like to get dressed up for work in my middle years and I feel prepared and confident when I do. A cup of coffee is also a must for me at work. I will literally pour a fresh cup, hold it in my hand and walk around for meetings or doing whatever teacher tasks I have, including actually teaching. Those are all things that I developed to go along with good work habits, and I've become ultra-efficient at work over the years.

You can do the same. Maybe you even select a song to wake you up to begin your new life habit with music that will signal your brain that there is something new going on and you can begin to associate the song with your new, healthy habits. Maybe you need something else to prime your new habits. Find something that you can associate your new behavior with and use it or wear it or listen to it consistently.

You may not get through your entire new schedule right away and that's ok. Get as far as you can each day and then try again the following day. Each day try to get a little further than you did before. Make sure you're as consistent as possible for as many consecutive days as possible but don't get discouraged. Changing your life for the better is an ongoing and difficult process. You're going to struggle at times. You're going to fail at times. Keep telling yourself that you're worth the effort and that you are going to be much healthier and happier when you develop the discipline to live the way you want; the way you deserve to live.

After working on your new habits and living your improved life for a couple of months, you may need to reevaluate. Are all the habits and behaviors you committed to helping? Do you still want to keep all of them? You'll probably find that everything you thought you wanted to do when you first made your schedule, is not as beneficial as you imagined. There may be a task or two or even more you want to substitute for something else. You may find that a habit you thought you only needed 30 minutes for you now want to dedicate an entire hour to.

The point is, even though you are working on writing out and sticking to a schedule to live a fuller life, it can be changed whenever you feel you know how to improve it. So, feel free to make some changes as you go until you are maximizing your time and living a life filled with joy. It will take time to incorporate everything you want into your schedule, but it will be worth it.

Review

- Highly successful people have healthy habits
- You will be more joyful if you adopt healthy mindsets
- Design your ideal schedule so you can imagine what your life looks like
- Begin to make the changes to your habits
- Associate things to help prime your brain to the new habits
- Keep working on living your new healthy life every day and never give up

Self-Work:

You need to list some new habits you want to try in an effort to improve your life. Brainstorm some changes you can make to your daily or weekly routine and even justify why you want to make those changes in your habit. Look back at your values, dreams and goals. Think about what habits would support those. You dream of being a best-selling author and have a goal of publishing a book in six months? Then you need to make a habit of writing every day, or at least scheduling time during the week for writing. You have a dream of running a marathon and a goal of losing weight? Then you need to make of habit of exercising. You get the point. Use what you've already done to help make some new habits.

Once you have a list of habits you want to include in your life, create an actual schedule. Make a schedule for a typical day. Then make a schedule for your week. And I get it, many of you hate schedules and lists. I do too! I have been, and would love to continue to be a "go with the flow" type of dude, but I finally decided I needed to be more productive and successful and last year I published two full novels with a short story out as well and now I'm super focused on inspiring and coaching people so I have to be disciplined! You need it as well so make that schedule!

Once you have your schedule now it is time to try to live it. It will take time and do not get discouraged. If you need to make small changes at first and build to a whole disciplined dynamic productive life, then that's what you have to do, but you have to start somewhere. Also remember to trick your brain into making new habits by using priming or associating something with your new habits like music or a beverage or a physical activity or something so that your brain can begin to get very used to the new you! It's going to be awesome and in no time you're going to be an even better version of the amazing person you already are!

Conclusion

You did it! You're on your way to a better you. You deserve to live a life of joy and contentedness. The only way to do that is to live your authentic life. If you ever feel off like something is just not right, stop and think about all the things you learned here. If you need to go back through and begin again to try to find what's wrong, I highly recommend that. You will often come to points in your life when things just aren't working and that often means you're not being true to yourself and not living true to your values. It's ok when that happens. It honestly will no matter how awesome you are and how amazing you are living. We live, we grow, we reach new stages of life and change and so we will feel out of place for that time and place and it is merely an opportunity to look at who we are again and make the changes to live our best life.

After reading this you now have a better idea of how to do that. Do not betray yourself and what you want. Love yourself and respect yourself enough to live the life you deserve. Now that you've identified what you've been doing, what you were currently doing and what you want to do you can move forward. There is a lot of work to do but it is worth it.

Keep your values close at hand and review them after some time. You may find that they change. Look at your goals and dreams every day so you do not forget what you're working towards. Continue to battle to keep your daily schedule aligned with all this new wisdom you have. Use the new tools and new motivation to work, a little bit at a time, at being a better you. You can do it but only you have the power to change. No one can do it for you. If you don't progress, ask yourself what you're doing to prevent growth. Make sure you love yourself enough to be better.

Great things are in store for you! Work towards them!

For more inspiration and coaching, and to book private coaching or sign up for seminars, please visit:

www.crazycoaching101.com

More books in the *This is Crazy!* Series coming soon!

Made in the USA
Coppell, TX
20 January 2021

48497177R00069